Towards Humanity

SHIFTING THE CULTURE OF ANTI-RACISM ORGANIZING

TAWANA "HONEYCOMB" PETTY

Edited by: Jamii Tata

1 Introductory Essay

2 Curriculum

3 Suggested References

Introduction

After years of engaging in various forms of anti-racism organizing, I discovered that the methods that were being used lent to further dehumanization of many parties involved, including myself. I was no longer comfortable participating in organizing that reinforced the hierarchal narrative of privilege, as I felt it to be false. I also felt that it did not allow well-meaning white anti-racist organizers to focus on their own humanity in the process.

I developed this curriculum with the hopes that we could embark on a new, more humane discussion. One that is premature, yet bursting with potential.

Through the combination of essays, suggested readings, film viewings and discussions, learners should have a thorough understanding of the system of white supremacy, racism, anti-racism organizing and how to shift the privilege narrative.

1st Edition – Self-published in January 2018

Edited by: Jamii Tata

1. Anti-racism Organizing: Demystifying the Privilege Narrative

Anti-racism Organizing Has Gotten Stale: Moving from Ally to Co-Liberator

During this period in my life, I have found myself committed to participating in anti-racism organizing efforts that move beyond black people and other people of color trying to convince white people that they have privilege and white people admitting to that privilege.

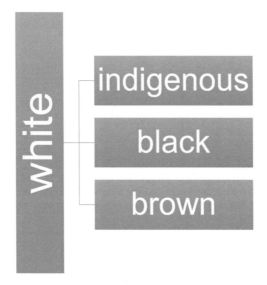

Figure 1 shows racial hierarchy

Those of us committed to anti-racism organizing need an entirely new conversation, one that has white people digging deeper into the impact racism has had on their own humanity. Drug abuse, domestic violence, suicide, mass murders, etc., are results of the same system that causes intraracial violence within black and brown communities.

I recognize that it is difficult for many to accept that the conditions faced by whites are tied to racism. Racism is a painful existence for blacks and other people of color, and anti-black racism is a deeper level of racism that blacks face, even within "allied" relationships.

As a black woman born and raised in Detroit, Michigan, a city that has suffered under a half-century of propaganda assault because of its predominately black racial demographic, I cannot ignore the impacts of anti-black racism. Anti-black racism has had a direct psychological impact on me and I have witnessed the impact it has had on my city, my entire life.

However, as I have begun to envision and work towards trying to realize the type of world I wish to live in, I have taken note of the impact that participating in such a dehumanizing system has had on well-meaning whites.

Although too many deny it, it has also become easy to take stock of the visible correlation between racism and capitalism.

When whites go into banks and other institutions, that have built their wealth on the selling of black bodies through slavery, and are afforded loans and other resources that are quite often denied to the descendants of slaves, this is an obvious connection between racism and capitalism.

When black and brown residents are uprooted from their neighborhoods and their homes replaced with stadiums and upscale hotels or businesses that cater mostly to a white population, those are obvious connections between racism and capitalism.

Figure 2 shows racial pursuit of the American Dream

But, what is less obvious is the psychological impact participating in this capitalistic racism has had on whites. The imaginary bubble that one must create around themselves in order to falsify a peaceful (often suburban) existence from the undesirable (black and brown) population, lends to a level of dehumanization in white people that many don't speak about.

Instead of confronting these realities in a systemic way, blacks, other people of color, and whites have allowed themselves to participate in a seesaw that reinforces a false hierarchical narrative. Black people and other people of color are on one side of the seesaw and whites are on the other side. This false dichotomy is the privileged and underprivileged seesaw.

This type of rhetoric cannot exist within anti-racism organizing. It will not create the world many of us wish to live in someday. It is the dominant narrative, not the counter-narrative. We need to be committed to the counter-narrative.

If white people don't begin to look at the impact the system of white supremacy has had on white people, those who have committed themselves to anti-racist organizing will continue to pursue undoing racism as a pet project they can pick up and put down. Undoing racism has to become a lifelong commitment white people make in order to humanize themselves. It cannot be something they do in the black community. Racism is not a black and brown community problem. Racism is something that is inflicted upon the black and brown community.

It is true that unarmed white people are not being gunned down by racist police the way that black people and other people of color are being gunned down. It is true that white people are not being redlined in order to allow for blacks to move into their neighborhoods. It is true that white school districts are not suffering massive school closings and disinvestment at a level that you see happening in black and brown neighborhoods. The system of white supremacy and the policies that are enacted in order to continue that system are vicious and unyielding, and we must do everything in our power to struggle against those policies and supporting forces. In order to do that, we need everyone in the struggle for racial justice to be doing so. This is why forcing well-meaning white people to shrink under white guilt and the false notion of privilege serves the movement for racial justice no real purpose.

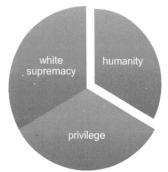

Participating with the system of white supremacy is far from a privileged existence. It is a dehumanizing existence. The further connected one is to a system that forces you to look through people based on their racial identity in order to survive or thrive, the farther away from your humanity you have to be.

Climbing the perpetual ladder to the American Dream requires a level of disconnect from what it means to be human that can only be nurtured with larger metal gates, deeper car garages, smaller front porches, and minimal contact with people all around you — even people who look like you.

Figure 3 shows disconnect from humanity

Is it truly a privilege to be connected to a legacy of lynching, displacement, redlining, etc.? We need new language. We need to pull away from the cycle of ally-ship and begin struggling towards co-liberation. We need whites to firmly believe that their liberation, their humanity is also dependent upon the destruction of racism and the dismantling of white supremacy.

This framing is new and challenging for our movement, but it is one that must be considered if we are truly to avoid revisiting the dynamics we are currently facing in this country another fifty years from now. It's time we recognize that true anti-racism organizing means that we must help each other down from the seesaw.

2. Undoing Privilege: Curriculum

Towards Humanity: The Shift

Topic: Shifting the narrative of privilege and strengthening anti-racism organizing.

Target Audience: Teens and adults of all ages interested in deepening their anti-racism organizing knowledge and skills while shifting the frame from ally-ship to co-liberation.

Brief summary of teaching strategy: Utilizing films, readings, podcasts, lectures and discussions focused on the history of white supremacy, racism, and other forms of social justice resistance in order to shift the narrative of privilege and strengthen anti-racism organizing.

After this unit of study, learners will be able to:

- Gain a greater understanding of the privilege narrative and how it came to be.
- Understand and articulate what white supremacy is as well as the various social forces that contribute to enforcing it.
- Utilize essays, films and suggested readings in order to identify and strengthen the counter-narrative(s) in anti-racism organizing.
- Recognize and struggle through contradictions as they arise in anti-racism discussions.

This unit will be broken into three segments:

1. The first and second segments consist of essays focused on how the "privilege" framework has contributed to a false hierarchal narrative that further dehumanizes all parties involved. Through reading the essays, learners will garner an understanding of the origins of the privilege narrative, as well as an understanding of the significance of the counter-narrative.

2. The third segment consists of several films and readings that learners should watch and then dissect in group discussions in order to deeper understand the origins of white supremacy, racism and deepen their anti-racism organizing.

3. All three segments consist of questions learners will need to engage in, in order to strengthen their analysis and anti-racism organizing strategies.

2.1 DIGGING DEEPER:
BEYOND THE PRIVILEGE NARRATIVE

Violence is Not Privilege, It's Detriment.

I'm not writing this as someone who has always thought this way. I wrote an entire poem around privilege in my book _Coming Out My Box_ in 2016. However, my thinking has since evolved. The urgency to be free of the system of white supremacy has become even more prevalent.

My mind can no longer connect a violent, oppressive and genocidal system such as white supremacy, with privilege. I can no longer encourage potential co-liberators to accept their history and collaboration with this system as a privilege. For me, accepting the ongoing legacy of trauma inflicted on blacks and other people of color as a privilege is dehumanizing for all involved. In fact, the terms privilege and ally within the anti-racist organizing movement have been so watered down that mentions of them make me a bit nauseous and triggered at times.

If someone snatched a child and raped and killed them, would we tell them to admit that they had the privilege of being with that child? Why then would we encourage well-meaning white people who hope to grasp the magnitude of slavery and the current system of white supremacy, to identify their connection to that violent history and current brutality as a privilege? Why are we framing white supremacy as a benefit from our Ancestors' brutal history of torture (many of whom were children)? Why are we framing it as a perk to benefit from our ongoing displacement and marginalization in this country?

Even with the resources gained and protections afforded by the system, based on whiteness, I would much rather hear white co-liberators say, "I recognize my detriment. I am actively struggling against white supremacy, here is how . . .". Because to identify with those gains with such affirmative language is detrimental to healing and progression in this country. It is detrimental to any real systemic change. If we reframe the connection to this brutality as a detriment, rather than a privilege it removes the optional ally-ship that is so prevalent within anti-racism organizing. If white co-liberators can see their connection to the legacy of slavery, lynching, redlining and other forms of racial violence as a detriment to their humanity, rather than a privilege to their existence, we can begin to balance the racial seesaw a bit.

whites

blacks/poc

Figure 4 seesaw shows perceived racial hierarchy

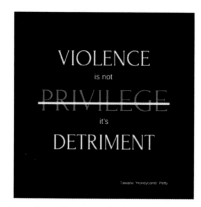

VIOLENCE
is not

~~PRIVILEGE~~

it's

DETRIMENT

Tawanё "Honeycomb" Petty

The argument around privilege versus detriment has been used in the past to think about how whites and blacks relate to the system of white supremacy. However, in those instances, the argument has been that we should refrain from calling white people privileged and instead identify black people as having the detriment. My argument is that this still reinforces the historical hierarchal narrative that got us here in the first place. It is a narrative that makes it a global phenomenon to consistently fail to recognize blacks and other people of color as fully human. I am also arguing that it is the indoctrination into the system of white supremacy and the connectedness to a legacy of violence and brutality towards human beings based on race, that is the actual detriment. Rather than determine a person's value (privileged or underprivileged) based on what one of my comrades would call, *stuff and status*, we can begin to reconnect morality with humanity.

It is a mistake to continue to teach black children and other children of color, even those who are without basic necessities, that they are underprivileged. We must begin to take care of their spirit. Society has already told them that they are less than, that they are hopeless and helpless. We must teach them that as we struggle against these systems that seek to dehumanize them, we

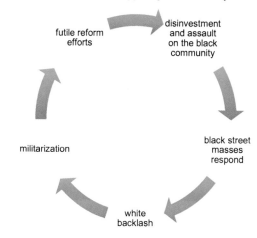

recognize their full humanity and will do everything in our power to strengthen and restore our villages, so that they don't have to go without.

Dr. King said, "True compassion is more than flinging a coin to a beggar; it comes to see that an edifice which produces beggars needs restructuring." I firmly believe that we all have greater control over the edifice than we have allowed ourselves to believe.

Figure 5 shows never-ending racial disparity

2.1 Questions:

Here are a few questions to get your juices flowing. Be sure to think of your own.

1. Why does the narrative white privilege no longer serve anti-racism organizing?
2. Why should the privilege narrative be considered as more of a detriment than a privileged existence?
3. What impact does the privilege narrative have on the humanity of people who identify as white?

Be sure to incorporate at least one related film, video, podcast or reading from the selected resources section.

2.2 Shifting the Language: From Ally to Co-liberator

The Testimony of Privilege

If you are a black person or another person of color, I am asking you to participate in ushering in a new narrative. I am asking you to relinquish your pursuit of white people as privileged beings. If you are a white person, I am asking you to relinquish the narrative that you live a privileged existence.

For those of you who made it through that first paragraph, we are well on our way towards visioning a more humane society. A society that allows everyone to show up in the conversation with their full humanity.

Discarding the narrative of privilege is not an invitation to ignore the brutality that black people and other people of color endure under the system of white supremacy. It's an invitation to contribute to a dialogue that moves us beyond the false dichotomy of hierarchy we have been unintentionally fostering through our anti-racism organizing. It is an invitation to recognize the more connected to our humanity we become, the less we will tolerate the dehumanization of others.

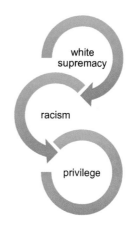

I have participated in dozens of mixed-race discussions around racism that left me feeling even more dehumanized than I felt before the discussion began. I have witnessed testimony after testimony from white *allies* giving their white privilege testament under the auspices of acceptance by black people and other people of color into the anti-racism organizing circle. Not only did I leave feeling dehumanized, but I felt dehumanized for the white people who I believed came to the events either seeking their humanity, or in pursuit of some measure of transformation.

Figure 6 the cycle of white supremacy

It's complicated, I know. But, what has capitulating to the shrinking of blacks and other people of color as the underprivileged and elevating white people as privileged actually done for the struggle against racism, or the dismantling of the system of white supremacy? I am personally exhausted by what has begun to feel like scripted performances by all parties.

At one of the recent gatherings I spoke at, a woman who identified herself as white stood up to counter my challenge towards the white privilege narrative. She described the ability to let her son walk "safely" two doors down from their home as a privilege. I was grateful that she provided her analysis of privilege, as it provided an opportunity for a deeper dialogue. A dialogue that moves beyond the misconception that there is some sort of magic bubble that protects you from the suffering in society if you just move far enough into the suburbs. One that removes the misconception that there is no suffering in the suburbs. A dialogue that challenges white people to take a deeper look at the impact racism and living up to the backwards standards of white supremacy has on them. A dialogue that interrogates the sort of survival that encourages you to disconnect from the "others" of the world in order to have the perception you are moving up in it. (see Figure 7)

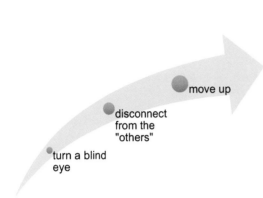

Figure 7 the road to dehumanization

The ways we have been identifying privilege are very limited in scope. The privilege narrative does not take into consideration the rich history and culture that has been historically and actively practiced in black, brown and indigenous communities. A culture that is consistently borrowed by the mainstream while the people whose culture it belongs to are hated by that very same mainstream. The privilege narrative negates the perseverance and stick-to-itiveness that black people and other people of color have demonstrated to the world through some of the most inhumane conditions inflicted upon us. The privilege narrative invisibilizes the ingenuity, artistry, creativity and *"make a way out of no way,"* resilience that blacks and other people of color have employed in order to survive in a society that till this day has failed to recognize us as fully human. But, even with all the social ills inflicted upon us, we are not underprivileged. I'm not claiming that existence any longer.

That fact that black, brown and indigenous humanity has been subjected to the interpretation of a society that suffers from the detriment of white supremacy is an even greater reason not to succumb to that analysis. Enough is enough. We have known the brilliance of black people and other people of color for long enough. There is no reason to keep pleading with anyone to recognize us as human.

What is imperative now is that we stand together in our power to shift the language and the narrative, and encourage those co-liberators who are serious about struggling against racism and dismantling the system of white supremacy, to shift their language and analysis as well.

We will not rid the world of all the 'isms that plague us by shrinking to them. None of us will.

Here's a quote from powerful Ancestor, Fred Hampton.

> "Black people need some peace. White people need some peace and we're gonna have to struggle religiously to bring about some peace because the people we're asking for peace, they are a bunch of meglamaniac war mongers! And we got to struggle with them to make 'em understand what peace means!"

It's time we moved onward and upward, together!

2.2 Questions

Here are a couple of questions to get your juices flowing. Be sure to think of your own.

1. Why should white anti-racist organizers shift from being allies towards co-liberators?
2. Why should black people and other people of color refrain from calling white people privileged?

Be sure to incorporate at least one related film, video, podcast or reading from the selected resources section.

2.3 The Call to Co-Liberate

Our Obligatory Opportunity

We have an incredible opportunity in 2018 and beyond to do things differently, more humane. My consistent call to all anti-racist organizers to pull away from the privilege narrative and to shift the language from ally to co-liberator is not merely a matter of semantics. It is an actual call to shift the culture of anti-racism organizing. It's a call to shift the way we view and treat one another.

A white person who views a black person or other person of color as something to ally with is more than likely going to view that person as inferior, someone to attempt to humanize. A black person or other person of color who views a white person as an ally is more than likely going to view that person as someone who has some control over their humanity.

We have enough historical and current knowledge to prove now that the *system* of white supremacy is backed by policies, procedures, practices, and propaganda that enforce and reinforce the white superiority narrative. We no longer have to feed it into though.

Anyone interested in reaching a deeper level of their humanity, especially under this current presidential administration is likely questioning the constant bombardment of propaganda that enforces the false dichotomy of black and brown as evil and white as pure. This age-old adage has run its course. Aspiring co-liberators around the world are struggling to figure out how we can more harmoniously co-exist together while preserving our dignity and culture. When we are forced to conform to individualism, extreme materialism and militarism in order to preserve our stuff and status, we are forced to disconnect from the hearts of the world we long to grow deeper connections with.

No doubt that the origins of white people's acceptance, and black and brown people's enforcement of the privilege narrative had mostly noble intentions. However, words have power. So, the decades long lack of consistent political education around the subject, coupled with the interpretation and embodiment of the word has led to an unintentional badge of honor. Instead of the term privilege being utilized as an avenue to dismantle oppression, it has turned into an aspiration for those who don't have it. A hamster wheel with no true potential to grow anything but more hamsters on the outside longing to get on the wheel. It's time to hop off the never-ending pursuit of the hamster wheel. The future of humanity depends on us shedding the sort of individualism that has us turning a blind eye to a world of suffering. It also depends on us figuring out how to live meaningful lives without demeaning the lives of others. I have faith that many hearts are up for the challenge.

2.3 Questions

Here are a couple of questions to get your juices flowing. Be sure to think of your own.

1. What is the origin of white privilege?
2. What are some opportunities you see for shifting the culture of anti-racism organizing?

Be sure to incorporate at least one related film, video, podcast or reading from the selected resources section.

3. What I Watched, Listened to and Read

Suggested Resources

Below is a series of films, videos, podcasts and articles that were considered in preparation for this curriculum. Some of the suggestions below are listed for historical purposes, others are suggested in order to showcase various opinions. Listings are not endorsements of views. In fact, some I outright disagree with, but felt they were significant enough to share because they aren't rare opinions. I won't make the point of identifying which resources I agree with, semi-agree with, or disagree with, because the purpose of this curriculum is to shift the paradigm.

A lot of the propaganda and literature created to date will lend to the rationale that white people indeed live a privileged existence. I am optimistic that this curriculum is a start to helping us transcend this argument and foster a movement towards a more humane version of humanity. A version of humanity that recognizes that further indoctrination towards the hamster wheel pursuit of the American Dream (the burning house Dr. King referenced), can no longer be considered a privilege, if we are honest with ourselves.

It is imperative that we study history and listen to varying perspectives in order to move the dialogue forward. There are many, many other resources out there. This is a very short list. Please do additional research for yourself.

Films/Videos/Podcasts:

1. Slavery by Another Name – Sheila Curran Bernard (available on PBS)
2. 13th – Ava DuVernay
3. American Revolutionary: The Evolution of Grace Lee Boggs – Grace Lee
4. The Unequal Opportunity Race (short video) – Erica Pinto (commissioned by the African American Policy Forum
5. Vincent Harding: African Americans and the American Dream (WGBH Forum – YouTube)
6. Vincent Harding: Creating America (Children's Defense Fund – YouTube)
7. Michelle Alexander: Locked Out of the American Dream (Moyers & Company – YouTube)
8. RACE – The Power of Illusion – Parts 1-3 (PBS)
9. Separate and Unequal (Frontline)
10. In Search of History: The Night Tulsa Burned – Sean P. Geary and Mark Montgomery
11. Opening the Question of Race to the Question of Belonging – John A. Powell (Onbeing)
12. Eyes on the Prize (series PBS)
13. Black Mothers Keep Dying After Giving Birth. Shalon Irving's Story Explains Why (All Things Considered)

Readings:

1. Uprooting Racism and Racists in the United States – James Boggs
2. Slavery by Another Name: The Re-Enslavement of Black Americans from the Civil War to World War II – Douglas Blackmon
3. Beyond the Wages of Whiteness: Dubois on the Irrationality of Antiblack Racism – Ella Myers
4. White Privilege and Male Privilege: A Personal Account of Coming to See Correspondences Through Work in Women's Studies – Peggy McIntosh
5. How 'Privilege' Became a Provocation – Parul Sehgal (The New York Times Magazine)
6. The Half Has Never Been Told: Slavery and the Making of American Capitalism - Edward E. Baptist
7. 5 Things About Slavery You Probably Didn't Learn in Social Studies: A Short Guide to 'The Half Has Never Been Told' – Braden Goyette (HuffPost Black Voices)
8. The Origins of "Privilege" – Joshua Rothman (The New Yorker)
9. What the Origin of 'Check Your Privilege' Tells Us About Today's Privilege Debates – Arit John (The Atlantic)
10. Checking My Privilege: The Character Basis of Privilege – Tal Fortgang
11. The Radical Work of Healing: Fania and Angela Davis on a New Kind of Civil Rights Activism – Sarah van Gelder (yes! Magazine)
12. Between the World and Me – Ta-Nehisi Coates
13. Racing into the Future – John A. Powell
14. Political Culture and Resurgent Racism in the United States – Maulana Karenga
15. Civil Rights & Black Identity – (The Atlantic)
16. How the News Media Distorts Black Families – Nicole Rodgers and Rashad Robinson (The Washington Post)
17. California's hidden homeless: Teachers, chefs, nurses and other middle class workers living in cars in parking lots because of the state's crazy property prices – Emily Crane (DailyMail.com)
18. On Racism and White Privilege (teachingtolerance.org)
19. Affluenza: How Overconsumption is Killing Us and How to Fight Back – John de Graff, David Wann, Thomas H. Naylor
20. In Detroit's comeback, many still being left behind, Detroit Future City report finds (Crains)

Deepening the Questions

Use the questions below and be sure to create your own.

"Sometimes the questions are more important than the answers."
– Grace Lee Boggs

1. What did you learn from the essays?
2. What are some ways you plan to shift the narrative around privilege in your anti-racism organizing work?
3. As a white person, what are some ways you plan to respond differently to the demand that you accept "privilege" as your identity?
4. As a black person or other person of color, what are some ways you plan to respond differently to calls for you to pursue white people as "privileged" beings?

Glossary

There are varying definitions to some of these terms, depending on the source. For the purposes of this curriculum guide, I am using yourdictionary.com.

Affluenza - Materialism or overconsumption in affluent societies, seen as a societal and environmental menace, as in large-scale consumer debt and product waste.

Ally - Ally is defined as an individual, country or organization that unites with another.

American Dream - An American ideal of a happy and successful life to which all may aspire.

Capitalism - The definition of capitalism is an economic system in which the means of production and distribution are privately or corporately owned and the operations are funded by profits.

Dehumanization - The act or process of dehumanizing.

Humanization - The act of humanizing.

Intraracial. Within race (group of people); of or by members of the same race

-Ism - a doctrine, theory, system, etc., esp. one whose name ends in *-ism*: a somewhat dismissive term

Liberation - Liberation is defined as being set free, or obtaining equal rights.

Mainstream - Mainstream is defined as the popularly accepted trends, ideas, principles and values that are accepted by the majority of people.

Narrative - any official or standard account or explanation, as of a sequence of related events

Pet project - A project, activity or goal pursued as a personal favorite, rather than because it is generally accepted as necessary or important.

Racism - Racism is a belief that one race is superior to the other or the practice of treating a person or group of people differently on the basis of their race.

Glossary continued.

Systemic - of or affecting a system, specif. an entire system

White supremacy - the social, economic, and political repression and exploitation of nonwhite peoples, esp. blacks, by white people, based on notions of racial superiority

White privilege - In critical race theory, a way of conceptualizing racial inequalities that focuses as much on the advantages that white people accrue from society as on the disadvantages that non-white people experience.

White guilt - A term used by some to describe the vacuum of moral authority surrounding whites on the issues of race due to their racial crimes against blacks.

Notes

Notes

Notes

Notes

Notes

About the Author

Tawana "Honeycomb" Petty is a mother, social justice organizer, youth advocate, poet and author. She was born and raised in Detroit, Michigan and is intricately involved in water rights advocacy, visionary organizing and digital justice work. Petty is the founder of Petty Propolis, a sponsored project of Allied Media Projects. She utilizes the various components of Petty Propolis to encourage creativity, re-spirit new and emerging artists of all ages, and nurture visionary potential through art, activism, facilitation and social justice organizing.

Petty is the author of Introducing Honeycomb, Coming Out My Box, and the Petty Propolis Reader: My Personal and Political Evolution. She is also a member and contributing writer of the Riverwise Magazine Collective and contributing blogger for Eclectablog.

She is a past recipient of the Spirit of Detroit Award, the Woman of Substance Award, the Women Creating Caring Communities Award, the Detroit Awesome Award, the Black Law Student Association's Justice Honoree Award, and was recognized as one of Who's Who in Black Detroit in 2013 and 2015. Petty is a board member of the James and Grace Lee Boggs Center to Nurture Community Leadership, a Data Justice Community Researcher for the Detroit Community Technology Project, a Detroit Equity Action Lab (DEAL) Fellow, a member of The Detroit Digital Justice Coalition and co-founder of the Our Data Bodies Project (ODB).

In addition to Petty's social justice and community organizing work, she performs and presents across the globe. She has appeared on several television and radio programs, including American Black Journal, Detroit Performs, Tavis Smiley and Stateside, and her work and writings have been featured in numerous publications.

Learn more about Tawana "Honeycomb" Petty at honeycombthepoet.org.